I thank God first for giving me the opportunity and willingness to write this book.

I also thank my beloved wife, Clarissa, for always being by my side, giving me support and strength so that this work could be completed.

Finally, I thank my precious daughters Ana Maria, Maria Ester, and Maria Clara, who make me wake up every day, always thinking about doing the best for them.

Cryptocurrencies Unraveled: Exploring the Future of Digital Finance

Cryptocurrency Course: From Invention to the Present Day

Module 1: Introduction to Cryptocurrencies

Module 2: Technology Behind Cryptocurrencies

Module 3: Top Cryptocurrencies

Module 4: Cryptocurrency Economics and Market

Module 5: Applications and Use Cases

Module 6: Regulation and Challenges

Module 7: Challenges and Controversies

Module 8: Future of Cryptocurrencies

Module 9: Future Prospects

Module 10: Practical Activities

Module 1: Introduction to Cryptocurrencies

History of Cryptocurrencies

- Emergence of the concept of cryptocurrency.

- The Bitcoin whitepaper by Satoshi Nakamoto.

- First Bitcoin transaction and the milestone of the purchase of two pizzas.

Emergence of the Concept of Cryptocurrency

Cryptocurrency arose from combining ideas about cryptography, economics, and computer science. Its roots can be traced back to movements by cryptographers and digital privacy enthusiasts in the 1980s and 1990s. They were looking for ways to create digital money that was secure, private, and decentralized, away from the control of governments and financial institutions.

The Bitcoin Whitepaper by Satoshi Nakamoto

In October 2008, a person or group under the pseudonym Satoshi Nakamoto published a whitepaper titled "Bitcoin: A Peer-to-Peer Electronic Cash System." This document was revolutionary in proposing a decentralized digital cash system based on blockchain technology. Key takeaways from the whitepaper include:

Decentralization: Bitcoin does not depend on a central authority. Instead, transactions are verified by a network of distributed nodes.

Blockchain: A public, immutable ledger recording all transactions in interconnected blocks.

Proof-of-Work: A consensus mechanism requiring miners to solve complex mathematical problems to validate transactions and create new blocks.

Digital Scarcity: Bitcoin's supply is capped at 21 million, creating a digital scarcity that can increase its value over time.

The Bitcoin whitepaper can be accessed here. https://bitcoin.org/bitcoin.pdf

First Bitcoin Transaction and the Milestone of Buying Two Pizzas

The first Bitcoin transaction occurred in January 2009, when Satoshi Nakamoto sent ten bitcoins to Hal Finney, a programmer and crypto enthusiast. However, the transaction that became a milestone in Bitcoin's history was the famous "purchase of the two pizzas."

On May 22, 2010, a programmer named Laszlo Hanyecz performed the first Bitcoin transaction for a physical good, buying two pizzas for 10,000 bitcoins. This event is widely celebrated in the cryptocurrency community as "Bitcoin Pizza Day." At the time, 10,000 bitcoins were worth about $41. Today, that value would be astronomical, demonstrating the massive appreciation that Bitcoin has experienced since then.

This transaction highlighted Bitcoin's potential as a medium of exchange and marked the beginning of its journey towards mainstream acceptance.

Getting Started

- Definition of cryptocurrencies.

- Difference between digital, virtual currencies, and cryptocurrencies.

- Blockchain: What it is and how it works.

Cryptocurrencies are digital or virtual currencies that use cryptography to ensure secure transactions. They operate decentralized through blockchain technology without the need for a central authority, such as a bank or government.

Difference Between Digital, Virtual Currencies and Cryptocurrencies

Digital Currencies:

- They are digital representations of traditional money.

- They can be issued by a central bank (such as China's Digital Yuan) or financial institutions.

- They are generally centralized and regulated.

Virtual Currencies:

- These are forms of digital money that are not issued or regulated by a government.

- Often used in specific environments, such as online games or social networks.

- They can be centralized (controlled by an entity) or decentralized.

Cryptocurrencies:

- They are a type of virtual currency that uses cryptography for security.

- They operate in a decentralized manner through peer-to-peer networks.

- Examples include Bitcoin, Ethereum, and Litecoin.

Blockchain: What it is and how it works

Blockchain is a technology that allows for the creation of a secure and immutable digital ledger.

How it works:

Blocks:

- A blockchain is made up of a series of blocks.

- Each block contains a set of recent transactions.

- A block also contains a hash of the previous block, creating a chain.

Mining:

- In the case of cryptocurrencies like Bitcoin, new blocks are added to the chain through mining.

- Mining involves solving complex mathematical problems to validate transactions.

Decentralization:

- The blockchain is maintained by a network of computers (nodes) spread worldwide.

- Each node has a complete copy of the blockchain.

- For a transaction to be added to the blockchain, most nodes must agree that the transaction is valid (consensus).

Immutability:

- Once a transaction is recorded in a block and added to the blockchain, it cannot be changed.

- This ensures the integrity and security of the data.

In summary, blockchain technology allows transactions to be carried out securely, transparently, and decentralized, making it the basis for the functioning of cryptocurrencies.

Module 2: Technology Behind Cryptocurrencies

Blockchain

- Block and chain structure.

- Block mining and network consensus.

- Types of blockchain: public, private, and hybrid.

Blockchain

Blockchain is the fundamental technology behind cryptocurrencies. It is a distributed, immutable digital ledger that records all transactions transparently and securely.

Blockchain

Blockchain is the fundamental technology behind cryptocurrencies. It is a distributed, immutable digital ledger that records all transactions transparently and securely.

Block and Chain Structure

The blockchain is made up of blocks of transactions, which are linked together in a linear sequence, forming a chain. Each block contains:

- Transaction Data: Information about the transactions made, such as Sender, recipient, and amount.

- Block Hash: A unique identifier generated from the block data. Any change in the data changes the hash, ensuring the block's integrity.

- Previous Block Hash: The hash of the previous block in the chain creates a link between the blocks, forming the blockchain.

Block Mining and Network Consensus

- Block Mining: Mining is the process by which new transactions are verified and added to the blockchain. Miners solve complex mathematical problems to find a valid hash for a new block. This process requires computational power and consumes energy. The miner who solves the problem first adds the block to the blockchain and receives a cryptocurrency reward.

- Network Consensus: The blockchain relies on a consensus mechanism to validate transactions and maintain the integrity of the network. Bitcoin, for example, uses Proof of Work (PoW), where miners compete to solve mathematical problems. Other mechanisms include Proof of Stake (PoS), where the probability of creating a new block depends on the amount of cryptocurrency the validator holds, and Delegated Proof of Stake (DPoS), where the community elects validators.

Types of Blockchain

- Public Blockchain: Open to anyone. Any individual can participate as a user, miner, or developer. Examples include Bitcoin and Ethereum. Security is guaranteed by decentralization and consensus mechanisms.

- Private Blockchain: Restricted to a specific group of participants. Permission to participate in and validate transactions is controlled by a central entity. Used by businesses to maintain privacy and control. Example: Hyperledger Fabric.

- Hybrid Blockchain: Combines elements of public and private blockchains. It allows selective control over who can participate in the network and access data. It offers the flexibility of private blockchain with the transparency and security of public blockchain.

Example: Dragonchain.

These blockchains are used according to each application's transparency, control, and security needs.

t

Security and Encryption

- Public and private key cryptography.

- Digital signatures.

- Digital wallets: types and how they work.

Security and Encryption

Cryptocurrencies' security is based on advanced encryption and authentication concepts, which ensure the integrity of transactions and the protection of users' funds.

Public and Private Key Cryptography

Public-key (asymmetric) cryptography is critical to the security of cryptocurrencies. It uses two types of keys:

- Public Key: A key that can be shared freely and is used to encrypt data. In cryptocurrencies, the public key serves as an address to receive funds.

- Private Key: A secret key used to decrypt data encrypted with the public key. The private key is used for cryptocurrencies to sign transactions and authorize funds transfers.

This key duo allows transactions to be secure and verifiable, ensuring that only the private key owner can move the funds associated with the public key.

Digital Signatures

Digital signatures are used to authenticate and verify the integrity of transactions. They guarantee that the rightful owner of the associated private key has authorized a transaction. The process of digital signature in cryptocurrencies involves:

Signature Creation: The owner uses their private key to create a digital signature for the transaction.

Signature Verification: Anyone on the network can use the Sender's public key to verify the signature. This confirms that the private key owner authorized the transaction without revealing the private key itself.

Digital Wallets: Types and How They Work

Digital wallets are used to store and manage cryptocurrencies. They contain public and private key pairs, making sending and receiving cryptocurrencies accessible. There are several types of wallets, each with its own security and convenience features:

Software Wallets:

• Desktop Wallets: These are installed on the computer and offer complete control over the private keys.
Example: Electrum.

• Mobile Wallets: Smartphone apps that allow for quick and easy transactions.
Example: Mycelium.

• Web Wallets: Accessible via a web browser. They are convenient but less secure, as third parties can control the private keys.
Example: Coinbase.

Hardware Wallets:

• Physical devices that store private keys offline. They offer high security against online hacks. Example: Ledger Nano S.

Paper Wallets:

• Physical printouts of public and private keys. Extremely secure against online attacks, but should be stored in a safe place to prevent loss or damage.

Multisignature Wallets:

• They require multiple private keys to authorize a transaction, increasing security. They are used by companies or groups that need shared control over funds.

Each type of wallet has its advantages and disadvantages, and the choice of wallet depends on the user's needs for security, convenience, and accessibility.

Module 3: Top Cryptocurrencies

Bitcoin
Altcoins

- Operation and protocol.

- Global market impact and adoption.

- Limitations and challenges.

Bitcoin

How Bitcoin works:

Bitcoin is a decentralized digital currency that allows peer-to-peer transactions without intermediaries like banks. Its operation is based on blockchain technology, a distributed ledger that records all transactions in a secure and transparent manner.

Bitcoin Protocol:

- Blockchain: The Bitcoin blockchain is a chain of blocks, where each block contains a set of verified transactions. Each block is cryptographically linked to the previous one through a hash, forming a chain.

- Mining: Mining is the process by which new transactions are added to the blockchain, and new bitcoins are created. Miners solve complex mathematical problems to find a valid hash for a new block. This process is called "Proof of Work" (PoW).

- Rewards: Miners are rewarded with new bitcoins and transaction fees when a block is successfully mined. The block reward is halved approximately every four years in an event called a "halving."

- Transactions: Transactions are initiated by sending an amount of Bitcoin from one wallet to another. Each transaction is digitally signed by the Sender, ensuring that only the private key owner can authorize the transfer of the funds.

Global Market Impact and Adoption

Impact:

- Financial Decentralization: Bitcoin revolutionized the concept of money by introducing a decentralized form of currency, where transactions are not dependent on a central authority such as a bank or government.

- International Remittances: Bitcoin has facilitated international money transfers, allowing for fast and low-cost transactions, especially for individuals in countries with underdeveloped or unstable banking systems.

- Store of Value: Many view Bitcoin as "digital gold," a store of value due to its limited supply (21 million bitcoins) and scarcity characteristics.

Adoption:

- Businesses and Retailers: Many businesses have started accepting Bitcoin as payment. Companies like Tesla and Microsoft have experimented with accepting Bitcoin payments.

- Institutional Investors: Financial institutions, hedge funds, and large investors have begun adding Bitcoin as an investment asset to their portfolios.

- Governments and Regulations: Some governments have adopted regulations to facilitate the legal use of Bitcoin, while others have banned or restricted its use due to money laundering and tax evasion concerns.

Limitations and Challenges

Scalability:

- Speed of Transactions: The Bitcoin network has a limited processing capacity, around seven transactions per second. This results in longer confirmation times during periods of high demand.

- Transaction Fees: Transaction fees can increase significantly during periods of congestion on the network, making small transactions unfeasible.

Security and Fraud:

- Hacking and Theft: Cryptocurrency exchanges and digital wallets can be targeted by hacker attacks, resulting in theft of funds.

- Loss of Private Keys: If a user loses their private key, they lose access to their bitcoins permanently, with no possibility of recovery.

Regulation and Adoption:

- Regulatory Uncertainty: The regulatory approach to Bitcoin varies widely between countries, creating uncertainty for users and businesses alike.

- Limited Acceptance: Although acceptance is growing, it is still limited compared to traditional fiat currencies.

Power Consumption:

- Mining: The mining process consumes significant energy, leading to environmental concerns. Most mining is carried out where energy is cheap, often generated from non-renewable sources.

Despite its challenges, Bitcoin continues to be an innovative force in the financial world. Its evolution and adaptation to market needs and future regulations will determine its role in the long term.

Altcoins

- Ethereum: smart contracts and the platform.

- Litecoin, Ripple, and other significant cryptocurrencies.

- ERC-20 tokens and the DeFi ecosystem.

Ethereum: Smart Contracts and the Platform

Ethereum:

Ethereum is a decentralized blockchain platform that goes beyond financial transactions by introducing the ability to create and execute smart contracts. It was proposed by Vitalik Buterin in 2013 and launched in 2015.

Smart Contracts:

• Definition: Smart contracts are computer programs that automatically execute, control, or document events and actions following the terms of a contract or agreement.

• How it works: These contracts run on the Ethereum Virtual Machine (EVM), a decentralized execution environment. They can be used for various applications like decentralized finance (DeFi), gaming, and voting systems.

Ethereum Platform:

• Ether (ETH): The native cryptocurrency of the Ethereum platform. It is used to pay for transactions and services within the network.

• Development: Ethereum allows developers to create decentralized applications (dApps) using the Solidity programming language.

Litecoin, Ripple, and Other Significant Cryptocurrencies

Litecoin (LTC):

• Origin: Created in 2011 by Charlie Lee, Litecoin is an alternative to Bitcoin, often called "digital silver."

• Features: Uses a different hashing algorithm called Scrypt, allowing for faster transactions and a block time of 2.5 minutes (compared to Bitcoin's 10 minutes).

Ripple (XRP):

• Origin: Launched in 2012 by Ripple Labs, Ripple is a platform and cryptocurrency (XRP) intended to facilitate fast and cheap international payments.

• Features: Ripple does not use traditional mining, and a consensus between network servers validates transactions. Financial institutions widely use it.

Other Significant Cryptocurrencies:

• Cardano (ADA): Focused on security and sustainability, it uses a consensus mechanism called Ouroboros (Proof of Stake).

- Polkadot (DOT): Enables interoperability between blockchains, facilitating communication between networks.

- Chainlink (LINK): An oracle protocol that allows smart contracts to interact with external data, bringing real-world information to the blockchain.

ERC-20 Tokens and the DeFi Ecosystem

ERC-20 tokens:

- Definition: ERC-20 is a technical standard for issuing tokens on the Ethereum blockchain. It facilitates the creation of new tokens that can interact with each other and with other smart contracts.

- Examples: Many popular tokens, such as USDT (Tether), USDC (USD Coin), and BNB (Binance Coin), are ERC-20.

Defi (Decentralized Finance) Ecosystem:

- Definition: DeFi refers to a set of financial applications built on blockchains, primarily Ethereum, that aim to recreate and improve traditional financial services in a decentralized manner.

- Components:

- Lending and Borrowing: Platforms like Aave and Compound allow users to lend and borrow cryptocurrencies.

- DEXs (Decentralized Exchanges): Uniswap and SushiSwap allow exchanging cryptocurrencies without intermediaries.

- Yield Farming and Staking: Users can earn rewards by providing liquidity or participating in transaction validation.

- Stablecoins: Cryptocurrencies pegged to stable assets, such as the US dollar, to minimize volatility (e.g., DAI, USDT).

The DeFi ecosystem is rapidly expanding, bringing innovation to the financial sector while presenting new regulatory and security challenges.

Module 4: Cryptocurrency Economics and Market

Cryptocurrency Savings

- Value and volatility.

- Limited supply and Bitcoin halving.

- Token models: utility tokens vs. security tokens.

Value and Volatility:

The value of cryptocurrencies is highly volatile, influenced by several factors, including:

- Supply and Demand: As with any market, the value of a cryptocurrency is determined by supply and demand. If demand increases and supply remains constant or decreases, the price rises, and vice versa.

- News and Market Sentiment: Government regulations, company adoption, and security issues (hacks, fraud) can cause large price swings.

- Speculation: Many investors buy and sell cryptocurrencies based on future expectations of appreciation, which can increase volatility.

- Technological Innovation: Advances in blockchain technology and new applications can increase the value of specific cryptocurrencies.

Bitcoin Limited Supply and Halving:

- Limited Supply: Bitcoin, for example, has a maximum supply of 21 million coins. This programmed scarcity is a crucial characteristic that influences its value. When demand grows while supply is limited, prices tend to rise.

- Bitcoin Halving: Halving occurs approximately every four years, and the reward for mining new blocks is halved. This slows down the rate of creation of new bitcoins, increasing scarcity. The halving tends to significantly impact the price of Bitcoin, often leading to price increases before and after the event due to the reduction in new supply.

Token Models: Utility Tokens vs. Security Tokens:

- Utility Tokens:

Definition: Utility tokens access products or services within a specific blockchain platform. They are not designed as investments but rather as a means of using a service.

Examples:

- Ethereum (ETH): Used to pay for transaction fees and services within the Ethereum platform.

- Basic Attention Token (BAT): Used to pay for advertising services on the Brave platform.

Use: Generally, these tokens are issued through ICOs (Initial Coin Offerings) to fund the development of a project.

- Security Tokens:

Definition: Security tokens represent an interest in an external asset, such as shares in a company, property, or debt. They are considered investments and are subject to securities regulations.

Examples:

- TZero (TZROP): Represents a stake in the tZero trading platform.

- Harbor (HRB): Used to tokenize real estate assets.

Regulation: Due to their investment nature, security tokens must comply with the securities laws and regulations of each jurisdiction, which may include registration, disclosure, and ongoing compliance.

Each token model serves different purposes and has different regulatory and usage implications. Utility tokens are more common in blockchain projects that seek to create new ecosystems or services, while security tokens represent traditional investments in a digitized way.

The cryptocurrency economy constantly evolves, with new token models and economic mechanisms emerging as blockchain technology advances and new use cases are explored.

Investing and Trading

- Cryptocurrency exchanges.

- Market analysis and trends.

- Investment strategies and risk management.

Cryptocurrency Exchanges:

Cryptocurrency exchanges allow users to buy, sell, and trade cryptocurrencies. There are two main types of exchanges: centralized (CEX) and decentralized (DEX).

- Centralized (CEX):

Examples: Binance, Coinbase, Kraken.

Features: Operated by companies facilitating cryptocurrency trading, offering liquidity, security, and customer support. Users must create accounts and undergo identity verification (KYC) processes.

Advantages: High liquidity, a wider variety of trading pairs, and advanced features like margin and futures trading.

Disadvantages: Users' funds are stored on the exchange, which can be a security risk in case of hacks.

- Decentralized (DEX):

Examples: Uniswap, SushiSwap, PancakeSwap.

Features: They operate without intermediaries, using smart contracts to facilitate direct user trading. They do not require registration or identity verification.

Advantages: Increased privacy, control over funds, and censorship resistance.

Disadvantages: Lower liquidity, the potential for errors in smart contracts, and generally less intuitive interfaces.

Market Analysis and Trends

Market Analysis:

Market analysis is essential for crypto investors and traders. There are two main approaches:

- Technical Analysis:

Definition: Focuses on studying historical price charts and market patterns to predict future movements.

Common Tools:

Technical Indicators: RSI (Relative Strength Index), MACD (Moving Average Convergence Divergence), Bollinger Bands.

Chart Patterns: Triangles, flags, heads and shoulders.

Objective: Identify market trends, entry and exit points, and price reversal signals.

- Fundamental Analysis:

Definition: Evaluate the intrinsic value of an asset based on factors such as project team, technology, use cases, adoption, and partnerships.

Criteria:

- Whitepaper: The clarity and feasibility of the project.
- Team: Experience and track record of the founders and developers.
- Partnerships: Strategic collaborations and support from institutional investors.

Market Trends:

• Market Cycles: The cryptocurrency market experiences bull and bear markets, which are influenced by factors such as technological innovation, regulations, and institutional adoption.

• Institutional Adoption: Growing interest and participation from financial institutions and businesses are driving the legitimacy and growth of the cryptocurrency market.

• DeFi and NFTs: Decentralized finance (DeFi) and nonfungible tokens (NFTs) are emerging sectors attracting significant attention and capital.

Investment Strategies and Risk Management

Investment Strategies:

• HODLing: Buying and holding cryptocurrencies for the long term, ignoring short-term volatility.
• Day Trading: Buying and selling cryptocurrencies within the same day, taking advantage of small price fluctuations.

• Swing Trading: Holding positions for a few days or weeks to capture intermediate price movements.

• Investing in ICOs/IDOs: Participating in Initial Coin Offerings (ICOs) or Initial Dex Offerings (IDOs) to acquire new tokens at low prices before they are listed on exchanges.

Risk Management:

• Diversification: Distribute investments among different cryptocurrencies to minimize risks specific to each asset.

• Stop-loss orders: Set auto-sell orders to limit losses on investment positions.

• Portfolio Allocation: Balancing the portfolio between high- and low-volatility cryptocurrencies and different asset classes such as Bitcoin, altcoins, and stablecoins.

• Research and Education: Staying informed about market developments, regulations, and new projects to make more informed investment decisions.

Investing in and trading cryptocurrencies involves significant risks due to their high volatility and complexity. A well-defined strategy and a disciplined approach to risk management are crucial.

Module 5: Applications and Use Cases

Smart Contracts

- Definition and examples.

- Implementation on Ethereum.

Definition:

Smart contracts are computer programs that automatically perform specific actions when certain predefined conditions are met. They operate on blockchain platforms, ensuring that the contract terms are fulfilled transparently and immutable without the need for intermediaries.

Examples of Use:

1. Decentralized Finance (DeFi):

Lending Platforms: Protocols like Aave and Compound allow users to deposit cryptocurrencies into liquidity pools and earn interest, while others can borrow using these funds as collateral. Smart contracts automatically manage loan and payment terms.

2. Insurance:

Automated Insurance Contracts: Platforms like Nexus Mutual use smart contracts to create decentralized insurance. When an insured event occurs (e.g., a delayed flight), the smart contract checks the relevant data and automatically pays the claim to the insured.

3. Real estate:

Transfer of Ownership: Smart contracts can be used to transfer real estate ownership in an automated manner. When the buyer sends the agreed amount of cryptocurrency, the smart contract automatically transfers ownership on the blockchain ledger.

4. Games and NFTs (Nonfungible Tokens):

Blockchain-Based Games: Games like Axie Infinity and Decentraland use smart contracts to manage the ownership and exchange of in-game digital assets, such as characters, items, and virtual land.

5. Logistics and Supply Chain:

Product Tracking: Smart contracts can track products along the supply chain. When a product reaches a certain point (e.g., a warehouse), the smart contract automatically updates the status on the blockchain, ensuring transparency and reducing fraud.

Implementation of Ethereum:

Ethereum is the most popular platform for implementing smart contracts. Developed by Vitalik Buterin and launched in 2015, Ethereum allows developers to create smart contracts and decentralized applications (dApps).

Features of the Ethereum Implementation:

1. Ethereum Virtual Machine (EVM):

EVM: The Ethereum Virtual Machine is the execution environment for smart contracts on the Ethereum blockchain. It ensures that all smart contracts run consistently and immutably across the network.

2. Solidity Programming Language:

Solidity: The primary programming language used to write smart contracts on Ethereum. Inspired by JavaScript and C++, Solidity is a high-level language that enables the creation of complex smart contracts.

3. Gas (Gas):

Gas Fees: "Gas" is a measurement unit used to calculate Ethereum network transaction fees. Each operation in a smart contract consumes a specific amount of gas, and users pay these fees in Ether (ETH). This encourages efficiency in the code of smart contracts and remunerates miners who validate and execute transactions.

4. Examples of Implementation on Ethereum:

Uniswap: A decentralized exchange (DEX) that allows the exchange of tokens directly between users without intermediaries. Smart contracts entirely operate it.

MakerDAO: A DeFi platform that allows the creation of the DAI stablecoin, collateralized by other cryptocurrencies. Smart contracts manage the process of collateralization and the issuance of DAI.

CryptoKitties: One of the first and most famous gaming dApps, allowing the creation, collection, and exchange of unique virtual cats, each represented by a smart contract on the blockchain.

Smart contracts have transformed the way transactions and agreements can be carried out, removing the need for intermediaries, increasing transparency, and ensuring automatic execution of agreed terms. Implementation of Ethereum, with its flexibility and robustness, continues to be a key pillar in the blockchain ecosystem.

Decentralized Finance (DeFi)

- What is DeFi?

- Examples of applications are lending, staking, and yield farming.

What is DeFi?

Decentralized Finance (DeFi) refers to an ecosystem of financial applications built on blockchain networks, especially Ethereum, that operate without traditional intermediaries such as banks and brokers. Using smart contracts, DeFi platforms execute financial transactions and agreements automatically when certain conditions are met. This provides greater transparency, security, and accessibility to financial services.

Application Examples

1. Lending

Platforms: Aave, Compound

Description: Users can lend their cryptocurrencies to other users and earn interest on those loans. In return, borrowers can obtain liquidity without having to sell their assets. Everything is managed by smart contracts that ensure the automatic execution of the loan terms.

2. Staking

Platforms: Ethereum 2.0, Polkadot

Description: Users "lock" their cryptocurrencies in a blockchain network to help ensure the security and operation of that network. In return, they receive rewards in the form of more cryptocurrencies. This process is essential in networks that use Proof of Stake (PoS) as a consensus mechanism.

3. Yield Farming (Agricultura de Rendimento)

Platforms: Yearn Finance, Uniswap

Description: Users provide liquidity to liquidity pools on decentralized exchanges (DEXs) and, in return, earn rewards in the form of transaction fees and additional tokens. Yield farming involves strategically moving funds between different pools to maximize returns.

Advantages of DeFi

Accessibility: Anyone with an internet connection can access financial services.

Transparency: All transactions are publicly recorded on the blockchain.

Interoperability: Many DeFi applications are compatible with each other, allowing for the creation of complex financial solutions.

Challenges of DeFi

Security: Smart contracts can have vulnerabilities that hackers exploit.

Regulation: Lack of regulation can lead to legal and compliance risks.

Complexity: New users may struggle to navigate the different platforms and understand the risks involved.

Decentralized finance represents a significant innovation in the financial sector, offering new opportunities and challenges for both users and regulators.

Other Use Cases

- NFTs and the digital art marketplace.

- Applications in supply chains, digital identity, etc.

NFTs and the Digital Art Marketplace

NFTs (Nonfungible Tokens) are cryptographic tokens representing ownership of a unique digital asset, such as art, music, videos, and collectibles. Unlike traditional cryptocurrencies, each NFT is unique and non-interchangeable. Platforms: OpenSea, Rarible, Foundation

Description: Artists can create and sell digital artworks directly to collectors without intermediaries. This democratizes the art market, allowing artists to exhibit and sell their works globally.

Example: Artist Beeple's "Everyday: The First 5000 Days" NFT auction, which sold for $69 million, is an emblematic example of the valuation of NFTs in the digital art market.

Advantages: Authenticity and provenance of works guaranteed by the blockchain, automatic royalties for artists in secondary sales.

Applications in Supply Chains

Blockchain can be used to track the origin, journey, and integrity of products along the supply chain.

Platforms: VeChain, IBM Food Trust

Description: Companies can record each step of producing and transporting goods on a blockchain. This provides transparency and reliability, helping to combat fraud and improve logistics efficiency.

Example: Walmart uses blockchain to track food, reducing the time it takes to trace the origin of a product from days to seconds.

Advantages: Increased transparency, reduced fraud, better quality control, and operational efficiency.

Digital Identity

Blockchain-based Digital Identity allows individuals to control their personal information and share it securely and verifiably.

Platforms: uPort, Sovrin

Description: Users can create secure, decentralized digital identities to access online services, verify credentials, and digitally sign documents.

Example: Countries like Estonia have implemented digital identity systems that allow citizens to vote, pay taxes, and access public services online securely.

Advantages: Full control over personal data, identity theft prevention, ease of credential verification.

Other Use Cases

1. Health

Description: Secure storage of medical records, improving interoperability between different health systems.

Platforms: Medicalchain, Patientory

2. Electronic Voting

Description: Secure and transparent voting systems, reducing voter fraud and increasing confidence.

Platforms: Voatz, Follow My Vote

3. Gaming

Description: Real ownership of digital game assets, such as characters, items, and virtual land.

Platforms: Axie Infinity, Decentraland

4. Energy

Description: Decentralized management of energy networks, allowing direct transactions between energy producers and consumers.

Platforms: Power Ledger, LO3 Energy

Blockchain is revolutionizing various industries by offering decentralized, transparent, and secure solutions that provide new levels of efficiency and trust.

Module 6: Regulation and Challenges

Legal and Regulatory Aspects

- Regulation in different countries.

- Compliance and KYC/AML.

Regulation in Different Countries

United States

Main Regulators: SEC (Securities and Exchange Commission), CFTC (Commodity Futures Trading Commission), FinCEN (Financial Crimes Enforcement Network).

Description: The SEC regulates tokens, which are considered securities, while the CFTC oversees digital assets such as commodities. FinCEN enforces anti-money laundering (AML) and Know Your Customer (KYC) regulations.

Challenges: Regulatory uncertainty about the classification of tokens and cryptocurrencies, causing concern among developers and investors.

European Union

Main Regulators: ESMA (European Securities and Markets Authority), EBA (European Banking Authority), FATF (Financial Action Task Force).

Description: The European Union is implementing the Markets in Crypto-assets Regulation (MiCA) to provide a clear regulatory framework for cryptocurrencies and tokens. In addition, AML and KYC guidelines are heavily enforced.

Challenges: Harmonization of laws between member states and adaptation of new regulations.

China

Main Regulators: PBoC (People's Bank of China).

Description: China has taken a strict approach, banning the trading of cryptocurrencies and ICOs (Initial Coin Offerings). However, it is actively exploring the use of blockchain for its digital currency, the digital yuan.

Challenges: Severe restrictions limit the growth of the cryptocurrency and DeFi market in the country.

Brazil

Main Regulators: Central Bank of Brazil, CVM (Securities and Exchange Commission), COAF (Council for the Control of Financial Activities).

Description: Brazil is developing cryptocurrency regulations, focusing on consumer protection, fraud prevention, and anti-money laundering.

Challenges: Lack of regulatory clarity can discourage innovation and investment in the sector.

Compliance and KYC/AML

KYC (Know Your Customer)

Description: Processes and procedures implemented by financial companies to verify the identity of their customers. This helps prevent fraud, money laundering, and other illegal activities.

Challenges: Implementing KYC on DeFi platforms is tricky, as they often operate decentralized without intermediaries.

AML (Anti-Money Laundering)

Description: A set of laws, regulations, and procedures to prevent criminals from laundering money through financial networks.

Challenges: The anonymous nature of many cryptocurrencies makes it difficult to enforce AML policies, requiring advanced technologies and international collaboration.

Additional Challenges

1. Safety

Description: Vulnerabilities in smart contracts and exchanges can be exploited by hackers, resulting in significant losses.

Solutions: Security audits, bug bounties, and the use of strict coding standards.

2. Scalability

Description: Many blockchains, including Ethereum, face scalability issues, resulting in high transaction fees and slowdowns.

Solutions: Layer-2 solutions such as rollups and sidechains and the transition to Ethereum 2.0 with Proof of Stake (PoS).

3. Interoperability

Description: Communication between blockchains is limited, making it difficult to exchange information and values between networks.

Solutions: Interoperability protocols like Polkadot and Cosmos allow interaction between multiple blockchains.

4. Market Adaptation

Description: The widespread adoption of blockchain and DeFi technologies is still in its early stages, with many people and businesses reluctant to adopt these new technologies.

Solutions: Education and awareness about the benefits and uses of blockchain, as well as the development of more user-friendly interfaces.

Regulation and compliance are essential for integrity and trust in the blockchain and DeFi ecosystem. However, balancing innovation with security and compliance remains a significant challenge for regulators and market participants.

Module 7: Challenges and Controversies

- Scalability and sustainability.

- Illicit use cases and fraud.

Scalability and Sustainability

Scalability Issues

Description: Many blockchains struggle to handle a large volume of transactions, resulting in network congestion, high transaction fees, and long processing times.

Example: The Ethereum network often faces congestion during periods of high demand, causing increased gas fees (transaction fees).

Solutions:

Layer 2 Solutions: Technologies such as rollups, state channels, and sidechains help improve scalability by

Scalability and Sustainability

Scalability Issues

Description: Many blockchains struggle to handle a large volume of transactions, resulting in network congestion, high transaction fees, and long processing times.

Example: The Ethereum network often faces congestion during periods of high demand, causing increased gas fees (transaction fees).

Solutions:

Layer 2 Solutions: Technologies such as rollups, state channels, and sidechains help improve scalability by

processing transactions outside the main blockchain and recording only the final results.

Sharding: Splitting the blockchain into multiple parts (shards) that can process transactions simultaneously, increasing the network's total capacity. Ethereum 2.0 is implementing sharding as part of its upgrades.

Sustainability

Power Consumption

Description: Many blockchains, especially those that use Proof of Work (PoW) as a consensus mechanism, consume large amounts of energy, raising environmental concerns.

Example: Bitcoin is often criticized for its high energy consumption, which is comparable to some countries.

Solutions:

- Proof of Stake (PoS): A consensus mechanism that is much more energy-efficient compared to PoW. Ethereum is migrating to PoS with Ethereum 2.0.

- Renewable Energy: Encourage using renewable energy sources for mining and operating nodes.

Illicit Use Cases and Fraud

Use for Criminal Activities

Description: Cryptocurrencies' pseudonymous and decentralized nature can facilitate illegal activities such as money laundering, terrorist financing, and illegal trading.

Example: Bitcoin use cases on the online black market, such as Silk Road, allowed anonymous transactions to purchase drugs and other illegal goods.

Solutions:

Regulation and Oversight: Implementing stringent regulations for DeFi exchanges and platforms, requiring KYC and AML.

Traceability Technologies: Advanced blockchain analytics tools like those developed by companies such as Chainalysis and CipherTrace help track suspicious transactions and identify illicit activity.

Fraud and Scams

ICO Scams and Rug Pulls

Description: Some cryptocurrency and DeFi projects have been used to defraud investors, such as Ponzi schemes, rug pulls (when developers abandon a project and steal investors' funds), and fraudulent ICOs.

Example: The DeFi project YAM faced a critical code glitch shortly after launch, resulting in significant losses for investors.

Solutions:

Due Diligence: Encouraging investors to conduct in-depth research on projects before investing.

Code Audits: Hiring specialized companies to audit smart contracts and DeFi project codes, increasing transparency and security.

Additional Challenges

1. Decentralized Governance

Description: Managing a network or project in a decentralized manner can lead to problems of coordination, voting, and implementation of changes.

Solutions: More effective governance models, such as DAOs (Decentralized Autonomous Organizations), allow for broader and more democratic participation.

2. Interoperability

Description: The lack of interoperability between different blockchains limits the transfer of assets and data between platforms.

Solutions: Interoperability protocols, such as Polkadot and Cosmos, that facilitate communication and information exchange between various blockchains.

3. Education and Adoption

Description: The technical complexity of blockchain and DeFi technologies can hinder mass adoption.

Solutions: Improve the user interface, provide education and training, and develop more user-friendly and intuitive applications.

The challenges and controversies associated with blockchain and DeFi are significant. Still, with continued innovation and collaboration between developers, regulators, and the community, many of these issues can be mitigated, allowing the technology to realize its transformative potential.

Module 8: Future of Cryptocurrencies

Trends and Innovations

- Second layer (Lightning Network).

- Cryptocurrencies and central banking (CBDCs).

Second Layer (Lightning Network)

Lightning Network

   Description: The Lightning Network is a second-layer solution designed for the Bitcoin blockchain, enabling faster transactions at lower costs. It works by creating payment channels outside the main chain, where multiple transactions can occur without recording each individually on the blockchain. Only the final balance is recorded on the main blockchain.

   Advantages:

   Speed: Almost instantaneous transactions.

   Cost: Significantly lower transaction fees.

   Scalability: Reduces congestion on the main blockchain, allowing for more transactions per second.

   Example: Used for micropayments and everyday transactions, allowing Bitcoin to be more practical for everyday uses.

Central Bank Cryptocurrencies (CBDCs)

CBDCs (Central Bank Digital Currencies)

   Description: CBDCs are digital versions of fiat currencies issued and regulated by central banks. They combine the convenience and security of cryptocurrencies with the trust and stability of government-issued currencies.
Advantages:

   Security: Issued by trusted monetary authorities, reducing the risk associated with private cryptocurrencies.

   Financial Inclusion: Facilitates access to financial services for people without access to traditional banks.

   Efficiency: Faster and cheaper transactions compared to traditional banking systems.

   Example:

   China: The digital yuan (e-CNY) is one of the most advanced examples of CBDC, and it has already been tested in several Chinese cities.

   European Union: The European Central Bank is exploring the digital euro, with plans to implement it in the coming years.

   Brazil: The Central Bank of Brazil is developing the Digital Real in the testing and public consultation phase.

Other Trends and Innovations

1. Interoperability

Description: To improve the ability of different blockchains and financial systems to communicate and transact with each other.
Example: Protocols like Polkadot and Cosmos lead this innovation, allowing different blockchains to operate together efficiently.

2. DeFi (Decentralized Finance)

Description: Continuing the expansion and sophistication of DeFi platforms, offering a more comprehensive range of financial services, such as loans, insurance, and derivatives, without intermediaries.

Example: Development of layer-2 solutions to improve the scalability and efficiency of DeFi platforms.

3. Asset Tokenization

Description: Physical and financial assets are transformed into digital tokens that can be traded on blockchains.

Example: Tokenization of real estate, stocks, and other traditional assets, increasing the liquidity and accessibility of financial markets.

4. Sustainability

Description: Development of more ecological and sustainable blockchain and cryptocurrency mining solutions.

Example: Ethereum's transition to Proof of Stake (PoS) with Ethereum 2.0 drastically reduces energy consumption compared to Proof of Work (PoW).

5. Regulation and Compliance

Description: Increased clarity and harmonization of regulations around cryptocurrencies and DeFi, providing a safer and more predictable environment for investors and businesses.

Example: Implementing regulations such as MiCA in the European Union, offering a clear framework for operating digital assets and DeFi platforms.

The future of cryptocurrencies is promising. Continuous innovations and the adaptation of new technologies promise to solve current challenges and further expand the potential of blockchain and cryptocurrencies. The interplay between regulation, technological innovation, and widespread adoption will be crucial in shaping the future landscape.

Module 9: Future Prospects

- Global economic impact.

- Possible technological evolutions.

Global Economic Impact

Financial Inclusion

Description: Cryptocurrencies and DeFi (Decentralized Finance) have the potential to provide financial services to unbanked or underbanked populations, especially in developing regions where access to traditional financial services is limited.

Impact:

Access to Credit: Facilitation of loans and microcredits.

International Transfers: Reducing costs and increasing the speed of international remittances.

Economic Empowerment: Access to new markets and investment opportunities.

Transformation of Financial Systems

Description: Cryptocurrencies encourage the modernization and digitalization of traditional financial systems, forcing banks and financial institutions to innovate and adopt new technologies.

Impact:

Efficiency: Reduction of operating costs and increased efficiency of financial transactions.

Transparency: Increased transparency in financial operations due to blockchain transactions' immutable and auditable nature.
Security: Improving security and reducing fraud through advanced encryption.

Adoption of CBDCs (Central Bank Digital Currencies)

Description: Implementing CBDCs by central banks could transform how money is distributed and used, providing a digital form of fiat currency that combines the benefits of cryptocurrencies with the stability of traditional currencies.

Impact:

Monetary Policy: Greater control over monetary policy and the ability to implement more effective economic measures.

Instant Payments: Facilitating instant payments and reducing intermediaries in financial transactions.

Systemic Risks: Potential changes to the structure of the traditional banking system, with commercial banks needing to adapt their business models.

Possible technological evolutions

Scalability and Efficiency

Description: Continued advancements in layer-two solutions (such as the Lightning Network) and scalability techniques (such as sharding and rollups) are crucial to enabling blockchains to support a higher volume of transactions without compromising speed or security.

Impact:

Mass Adoption: Increased ability to support large-scale adoption of cryptocurrencies for everyday uses.

Performance: Reducing costs and improving the performance of blockchain networks.

Interoperability

Description: Development of protocols that allow the communication and transfer of data and assets between different blockchains, facilitating the integration of various platforms and increasing the overall functionality of the ecosystem.

Impact:

Systems Synergy: Creating a more cohesive and functional blockchain ecosystem.

Flexibility: Greater flexibility for developers and users by combining functionalities from different blockchains.

Security and Privacy

Description: Advances in cryptography and privacy technologies (such as zk-SNARKs and zk-STARKs) will increase the security and confidentiality of blockchain transactions.

Impact:

Confidentiality: Enhanced protection of users' privacy.

Resilience: Reduced vulnerability to attacks and fraud.

Integration with Emerging Technologies

Artificial Intelligence (AI): AI and blockchain can improve data analysis, smart contract automation, and fraud detection.

Internet of Things (IoT): Integrating blockchain with IoT can create more secure and transparent systems for managing connected devices, such as in supply chains and smart cities.

Module 10: Practical Activities

- Creation of a Digital Wallet

- Configuration and security.

- Transaction Simulation

- Sending and receiving cryptocurrencies.

- Market Analysis

- Technical and fundamental analysis tools.

- Hands-On Crypto Activities

Creating a Digital Wallet

Configuration

1. Choice of Wallet Type:

Software Wallets: Desktop or mobile applications (e.g., Exodus, Electrum).

Hardware Wallets: Physical devices that store private keys offline (e.g., Ledger, Trezor).

Paper Wallets: Printing private and public keys on paper for offline storage.

2. Download and Install:

Download the official wallet software or buy a hardware wallet from a trusted source.

Follow the installation and configuration instructions provided by the developer.

3. Creation of the Portfolio:

Launch the wallet app.

Follow the setup process, which usually generates a new private key and a seed phrase.

Write down the recovery phrase and store it in a safe offline location.

Safety

1. Wallet Backup:

Store the recovery phrase in multiple secure, offline locations.

Regularly back up your wallet files, mainly if you use a software wallet.

2. Private Key Protection:

Never share your private key.

Use hardware wallets to store large amounts of cryptocurrencies, as they are safer from online attacks.

3. Two-Factor Authentication (2FA):

Enable 2FA for accounts associated with exchanges or online wallets.

Use authentication apps like Google Authenticator or Authy.

4. Software Updates:

Keep the wallet software and hardware wallet firmware up to date.

Transaction Simulation

Sending Cryptocurrencies

1. Obtaining the Recipient's Address:

Ask your recipient for their wallet address to send the crypto.

Check the validity and compatibility of the address with the currency you're sending to.

2. Start the Transaction:

Open your digital wallet.

Select the send option. Enter the recipient's address and the amount to send, and if applicable, adjust the transaction fees.

3. Confirmation:

Review all transaction information.

Confirm the transaction and enter any additional authentication required (e.g., password, 2FA).

4. Transaction Verification:

After confirmation, check the transaction status using a blockchain explorer (e.g., Etherscan for Ethereum).

Receiving Cryptocurrencies

1. Obtaining Your Address:

Open your digital wallet.

Copy your public address or use the QR code provided by the wallet.

2. Providing the Address to the Sender:

Send your public address to the Sender.

Verify the incoming transaction using a blockchain explorer.

Market Analysis

Technical Analysis Tools

1. Price Charts:

TradingView: Popular platform for technical analysis with detailed charts and indicators.

CoinGecko/CoinMarketCap: Provide historical price charts and market indicators.

2. Technical Indicators:

Moving Averages (MA): Trend indicators that smooth out price data.

Relative Strength Index (RSI): Measures the speed and change of price movements.

Bollinger Bands: Volatility indicators consisting of one moving average line and two standard deviation lines.

Fundamental Analysis Tools

1. Projects and Teams:

Research the background and reputation of the developers and team behind a cryptocurrency.

Evaluation of the whitepaper and project vision.

2. Adaptation and Use:

Analysis of cryptocurrency adoption, strategic partnerships, and use in real applications.

Monitoring relevant news and developments.

3. On-Chain Metrics:

Number of Active Addresses: Indicator of network activity and adoption.

Transaction Volume: Measure of cryptocurrency utilization and demand.

4. Market Sentiment:

Sentiment Analysis: Tools that analyze market sentiment based on mentions on social media, news, and forums.

Fear and Greed Indicators: These measure overall investor sentiment, and help identify oversold or overbought market conditions.

These hands-on activities, from securely setting up a wallet to in-depth market analysis, provide a solid foundation for exploring and understanding the workings and potential of cryptocurrencies.

Resources and Supporting Materials

- Recommended Readings

- Whitepapers, articles and books.

- Online Tools

- Blockchain explorers and market simulators.

- Communities and Forums

- Participation in online communities and events.

Recommended Readings

Whitepapers

Bitcoin: Bitcoin: A Peer-to-Peer Electronic Cash System by Satoshi Nakamoto. The original document that introduced Bitcoin and blockchain technology.

Ethereum: Ethereum Whitepaper. A document outlining the vision and technology behind the Ethereum platform.

Polkadot: Polkadot Whitepaper. It explains the architecture and goals of the Polkadot network.

Articles

"The Double-Spending Problem and Cryptocurrencies": This article explains how cryptocurrencies solve the double-spending problem.

"On Bitcoin and Red Balloons": Analysis of Bitcoin's security and efficiency properties.

Books

"Mastering Bitcoin" by Andreas M. Antonopoulos: A comprehensive guide to Bitcoin technology, suitable for beginners and developers.

The Bitcoin Standard" by Saifedean Ammous: Explores the economic and historical impact of Bitcoin as a new form of money.

"Blockchain Basics" by Daniel Drescher: Step-by-step introduction to the workings and potential of blockchain technology.

"Online Tools

Blockchain Explorers

Etherscan: An explorer for the Ethereum blockchain, it allows you to verify transactions, smart contracts, and addresses.

Blockchain.com: Explorer for Bitcoin, allows you to track transactions and view network statistics.

Polkascan: Explorer for the Polkadot network and its parachains.

Market Simulators

TradingView: Charting and technical analysis tool that offers trade simulation.
CoinMarketCap: Offers market data, including prices, volumes, and market capitalization of various cryptocurrencies.

Cryptohopper: Platform that allows simulation of automated trading with bots.

Communities and Forums

Participation in Online Communities

Reddit: Subreddits like r/Bitcoin, r/Ethereum, and r/CryptoCurrency are great for discussions, news, and updates.

Twitter: Follow crypto influencers, developers, and projects for the latest news and analysis.

Discord/Telegram: Many cryptocurrencies and DeFi projects have dedicated Discord servers and Telegram channels where community members can discuss developments and ask questions.

Events and Conferences

Conferences: Consensus, Devcon (Ethereum), and Bitcoin Conference bring together experts, developers, and enthusiasts to discuss the latest innovations and trends.
Meetups: Local groups often host meetups where crypto enthusiasts can gather, learn, and share knowledge.

Websites and Blogs

CoinDesk: One of the leading cryptocurrency news sites, providing analysis, news, and insights.

Medium: Many developers and projects publish technical articles and updates on Medium.

Summary

These resources and supporting materials provide a solid foundation for anyone who wants to understand and engage with cryptocurrencies and blockchain. From reading whitepapers and foundational books to participating in communities and using online tools, there is a wide range of options for deepening knowledge and practice in cryptocurrencies.

REFERENCE

1. Nakamoto, Satoshi. "Bitcoin: A Peer-to-Peer Electronic Cash System."
2. Buterin, Vitalik. "Ethereum Whitepaper."
3. Antonopoulos, Andreas M. "Mastering Bitcoin."
4. Ammous, Saifedean. "The Bitcoin Standard."
5. Drescher, Daniel. "Blockchain Basics."
6. Narayanan, Arvind, et al. "Bitcoin and Cryptocurrency Technologies."
7. Tapscott, Don, and Tapscott, Alex. "Blockchain Revolution."
8. Mougayar, William. "The Business Blockchain."
9. Hileman, Garrick, and Rauchs, Michel. "Global Blockchain Benchmarking Study."
10. Vigna, Paul, and Casey, Michael J. "The Age of Cryptocurrency."
11. Lewis, Danny. "The Double-Spending Problem and Cryptocurrencies."
12. Zohar, Aviv. "Bitcoin: An Innovative Alternative Digital Currency."
13. Eyal, Ittay, and Sirer, Emin Gün. "Majority is not Enough: Bitcoin Mining is Vulnerable."
14. Bonneau, Joseph et al. "SoK: Research Perspectives and Challenges for Bitcoin and Cryptocurrencies."
15. Kroll, Joshua A., Davey, Ian C., and Felten, Edward W. "The Economics of Bitcoin Mining, or Bitcoin in the Presence of Adversaries."
16. Gervais, Arthur et al. "On the Security and Performance of Proof of Work Blockchains."
17. Li, Xiaofan, and Palanisamy, Bhaskar. "Privacy in Decentralized Online Social Networks."
18. Al-Saqaf, Walid, and Seidler, Nicolas. "Blockchain Technology for Social Impact: Opportunities and Challenges Ahead."
19. Narayanan, Arvind, et al. "Bitcoin and Cryptocurrency Technologies: A Comprehensive Introduction."
20. Meiklejohn, Sarah et al. "A Fistful of Bitcoins: Characterizing Payments Among Men with No Names."
21. Miers, Ian et al. "Zerocoin: Anonymous Distributed E-Cash from Bitcoin."
22. Green, Matthew, et al. "Zerocash: Decentralized Anonymous Payments from Bitcoin."
23. Christidis, Konstantinos, and Devetsikiotis, Michael. "Blockchains and Smart Contracts for the Internet of Things."

24. Bashir, Imran. "Mastering Blockchain."
25. DuPont, Quinn. "Cryptocurrencies and Blockchains."
26. Benet, Juan. "IPFS - Content Addressed, Versioned, P2P File System."
27. Croman, Kyle et al. "On Scaling Decentralized Blockchains."
28. Bentov, Iddo, et al. "Proof of Activity: Extending Bitcoin's Proof of Work via Proof of Stake."
29. Lerner, Sergio Demian. "Bitcoin Economics: An Introduction and Survey."
30. Bonneau, Joseph, et al. "Mixcoin: Anonymity for Bitcoin with Accountable Mixes."
31. Biryukov, Alex, et al. "Deanonymisation of Clients in Bitcoin P2P Network."
32. Heilman, Ethan, et al. "Eclipse Attacks on Bitcoin's Peer-to-Peer Network."
33. Eyal, Ittay. "The Miner's Dilemma."
34. Ron, Dorit, and Shamir, Adi. "Quantitative Analysis of the Full Bitcoin Transaction Graph."
35. Andrychowicz, Marcin et al. "Secure Multiparty Computations on Bitcoin."
36. Reid, Fergal, and Harrigan, Martin. "An Analysis of Anonymity in the Bitcoin System."
37. Bonneau, Joseph. "Why Buy When You Can Rent? Bribery Attacks on Bitcoin-Style Consensus."
38. Nakamoto, Satoshi. "Bitcoin: A Peer-to-Peer Electronic Cash System."
39. Ali, Robleh, et al. "Innovations in Payment Technologies and the Emergence of Digital Currencies."
40. Berentsen, Aleksander, and Schär, Fabian. "A Short Introduction to the World of Cryptocurrencies."
41. Conoscenti, Marco, et al. "Blockchain for the Internet of Things: A Systematic Literature Review."
42. Crosby, Michael, et al. "Blockchain Technology: Beyond Bitcoin."
43. Mattila, Juri. "The Blockchain Phenomenon – The Disruptive Potential of Distributed Consensus Architectures."
44. Böhme, Rainer et al. "Bitcoin: Economics, Technology, and Governance."
45. Peters, Gareth W., and Panayi, Efstathios A. "Understanding Modern Banking Ledgers through Blockchain Technologies: Future of Transaction Processing and Smart Contracts on the Internet of Money."
46. Yermack, David. "Is Bitcoin a Real Currency? An Economic Appraisal."
47. Catalini, Christian, and Gans, Joshua S. "Some Simple Economics of the Blockchain."
48. Biais, Bruno, et al. "The Blockchain Folk Theorem."
49. Barber, Simon, et al. "Bitter to Better—How to Make Bitcoin a Better Currency."
50. Biryukov, Alex, and Khovratovich, Dmitry. "Equihash: Asymmetric Proof-of-Work Based on the Generalized Birthday Problem."
51. Bonneau, Joseph, et al. "Bitcoin and Cryptocurrency Technologies: A Comprehensive Introduction."
52. Chiu, Jonathan, and Koeppl, Thorsten V. "The Economics of Cryptocurrencies–Bitcoin and Beyond."
53. Gervais, Arthur, et al. "Is Bitcoin a Decentralized Currency?"
54. Halaburda, Hanna, and Sarvary, Miklos. "Beyond Bitcoin: The Economics of Digital Currencies."
55. Harvey, Campbell R. "Cryptofinance."

56. Hoffmann, Sebastian, and Zamyatin, Alexei. "An Analysis of Bitcoin's Proof of Work Mechanism."
57. Kiayias, Aggelos, et al. "Ouroboros: A Provably Secure Proof-of-Stake Blockchain Protocol."
58. Kiyotaki, Nobuhiro, and Wright, Randall. "A Search-Theoretic Approach to Monetary Economics."
59. Makarov, Igor, and Schoar, Antoinette. "Trading and Arbitrage in Cryptocurrency Markets."
60. Malinova, Katya, and Park, Andreas. "Market Design with Blockchain Technology."
61. Narayanan, Arvind, and Clark, Jeremy. "Bitcoin's Academic Pedigree."
62. Nofer, Michael et al. "Blockchain."
63. Saleh, Fahad. "Blockchain without Waste: Proof-of-Stake."
64. Tse, David, et al. "Blockchain Economics."
65. Vucolic, Marko. "The Quest for Scalable Blockchain Fabric: Proof-of-Work vs. BFT Replication."
66. Wei, William. "The Impact of Tether Grants on Bitcoin."
67. Xu, Mingxiao, et al. "Blockchain Technology: A Survey on State of the Art and Future Directions."
68. Wüst, Karl, and Gervais, Arthur. "Do You Need a Blockchain?"
69. Zarifis, Alex, et al. "Smart Contracts for Accounting Information Systems."
70. Zyskind, Guy, et al. "Decentralizing Privacy: Using Blockchain to Protect Personal Data."
71. Babenko, Maxim, and Sberbank. "The Impact of Blockchain on the Financial Sector."
72. Biswas, Kamanashis, and Muthukkumarasamy, Vallipuram. "Securing Smart Cities Using Blockchain Technology."
73. Choi, Hwa Young, et al. "The Application of Blockchain Technology in the Music Industry."
74. De Filippi, Primavera, and Wright, Aaron. "Blockchain and the Law: The Rule of Code."
75. Gupta, Manav. "Blockchain for Dummies."
76. Iansiti, Marco, and Lakhani, Karim R. "The Truth About Blockchain."
77. Kshetri, Nir. "Blockchain's Roles in Meeting Key Supply Chain Management Objectives."
78. Tapscott, Don, and Tapscott, Alex. "How Blockchain Is Changing Finance."
79. Werbach, Kevin. "The Blockchain and the New Architecture of Trust."
80. Xu, Xun, et al. "The Future of Smart Manufacturing: A Review Paper."
81. Yaga, Dylan et al. "Blockchain Technology Overview."
82. Zheng, Zibin, et al. "An Overview of Blockchain Technology: Architecture, Consensus, and Future Trends."
83. Bach, Laurent et al. "Consistent DDoS Protection with Programmable Switches."
84. Bennett, Megan, et al. "Building a Secure Decentralized Infrastructure."
85. Bonomi, Flavio, et al. "Fog Computing: A Platform for the Internet of Things and Analytics."
86. Chang, Victor, et al. "A Blockchain-Based Architecture for the Cloud of Things."
87. Chen, Ming, et al. "Big Data: Related Technologies, Challenges, and Future Prospects."
88. Christidis, Konstantinos, et al. "Survey on Blockchain and Its Applications in IoT."
89. Croman, Kyle et al. "On Scaling Decentralized Blockchains."
90. Grigg, Ian. "Triple Entry Accounting."
91. Nakamoto, Satoshi. "Bitcoin: A Peer-to-Peer Electronic Cash System."
92. Pilkington, Marc. "Blockchain Technology: Principles and Applications."
93. Schollmeier, Ralf. "A Definition of Peer-to-Peer Networking for the Classification of Peer-to-Peer Architectures and Applications."

I am a doctor, married, and father of three beautiful daughters.

I started studying and becoming interested in cryptocurrencies and blockchain 15 years ago.

This book, Cryptocurrencies Unraveled: Exploring the Future of Digital Finance, is structured to take you from the basics to the advanced concepts, with each chapter building on the previous one. Here, you will learn from scratch how to start your first transactions.

After two years of intense reading and research, I present this book suitable for beginners and the most experienced.

Have fun and learn a lot.

See you around